EDGE BOOKS™

HALLOWEEN EXTREME

HOW TO MAKE

Frightening Halloween Decorations

by Catherine Ipcizade

CAPSTONE PRESS
a capstone imprint

Edge Books are published by Capstone Press,
1710 Roe Crest Drive, North Mankato, Minnesota 56003.
www.capstonepub.com

Books published by Capstone Press are manufactured with paper
containing at least 10 percent post-consumer waste.

Library of Congress Cataloging-in-Publication Data
Ipcizade, Catherine
How to make frightening Halloween decorations / by Catherine Ipcizade.
     p. cm. — (Edge books. Halloween extreme)
Includes bibliographical references and index.
Summary: "Provides step-by-step instructions for making Halloween decorations
     using household materials"—Provided by publisher.
     ISBN 978-1-4296-5423-4 (library binding)
1. Halloween decorations—Juvenile literature. I. Title. II. Series.
TT900 .H32I63 2011
745.594'1646—dc22
                                                          2010030176

Editorial Credits
Megan Peterson and Angie Kaelberer, editors; Juliette Peters, designer;
     Sarah Schuette, photo stylist; Marcy Morin, project production;
     Eric Manske, production specialist

Photo Credits
All photos by Capstone Studio/Karon Dubke

Artistic Effects
Shutterstock/Merkushev Vasiliy, Randall Mikulas, Renee Reeder BFA

Printed in the United States of America in Stevens Point, Wisconsin.
122011   006527WZVMI

Table of Contents

Introduction

Is Halloween your favorite holiday? Do you like to scare people or gross them out? Then you've come to the right place! The pages of this book are filled with frightening and disgusting Halloween decorations.

Anyone can buy Halloween decorations at a store. But with this book, you can wow your friends and family by making them at home. Turn common household items like milk jugs and egg cartons into creepy creations. When you make your own Halloween decorations, you decide how spooky they'll be.

None of the decorations you're about to make will actually hurt anyone. A few projects are made with some **edible** ingredients, but don't dare your best friend to eat them. And make sure to ask an adult to help when working with dangerous items like a hot glue gun and dry ice.

edible—able to be eaten

Tools

electrical tape

scissors

glue gun

strainer

tongs

This spine-tingling book is just the beginning of all the fun projects you can make for Halloween. But be careful. Once your friends see your decorations, they might try to spook you next! So what are you waiting for? Turn the page, and let's get this Halloween party started.

Knock Knock!

You might have to dare your friends to open this freaky door. If the hairy spiders don't frighten guests, the scary signs will!

BEWARE

HERE LIES
TOM B. STONE

R.I.P.
SKIN E
BONES

BURIED A.
LIVE

What You Need:

- scissors
- 2 to 3 large black or orange trash bags
- masking tape
- gray and orange construction paper
- markers
- white glue
- cotton balls
- glue gun and glue sticks
- plastic spiders and bugs
- red acrylic paint

Step 1: Cut large trash bags down the middle so they lay flat. Cover the front of the door with the bags. Tape to secure.

Step 2: Use gray construction paper and markers to create a large "beware" sign. Tape it to the top of the door.

Step 3: Cut out pumpkins from orange construction paper. Use markers to draw scary faces on the pumpkins. Tape pumpkins to the door.

Step 4: Cut out mini headstones from gray construction paper. Use markers to write funny or spooky statements on the stones. Tape headstones to the door.

Step 5: Pull cotton balls apart and glue to the door. Hot glue fake spiders and bugs on top of the cotton.

Step 6: Cover your palm with red paint. Add "bloody" handprints to the door.

TIP: Does your front door have a window? Don't cover the window with the garbage bag. Instead, cut out a pair of spooky eyes from red construction paper. Tape the eyes in the window.

Witch's Brew

Surprise your friends with this eerie-looking drink. When water hits the dry ice, your brew will start to smoke. Tell your friends they're going into the pot next and watch them squirm.

What You Need:

- construction paper
- markers
- glue gun and hot glue
- gummy worms
- 1 large black plastic cauldron
- utility gloves
- 1 block dry ice
- tongs
- water
- punch bowl
- root beer
- ladle
- drinking cups

Step 1: Use construction paper and markers to create a spooky sign that lists the ingredients of your brew. Set aside.

Step 2: Hot glue gummy worms to the outside of a plastic cauldron. The worms should look like they're crawling out of the cauldron.

Step 3: Wearing utility gloves, carefully break up the ice with an ice pick or hammer if needed to make it fit. Have an adult place a block of dry ice into the bottom of the cauldron, using the tongs and utility gloves.

Step 4: Add just enough water to the dry ice to cover it. The ice will start to smoke.

Step 5: Place your punch bowl on top of the dry ice. Pour root beer into the punch bowl. Set the sign next to the cauldron.

Step 6: Use the ladle to pour the Witch's Brew into cups.

TIP: Work quickly after pouring water on the dry ice. Dry ice doesn't smoke for long. Also, never touch dry ice with your bare hands—it will burn your skin.

Glow-in-the-Dark Aliens

Convince people they're about to be abducted by aliens with this simple milk jug project. Place these spooky "heads" all over the house and yard. The little green men will have your friends searching for UFOs.

What You Need:

- paintbrush
- black acrylic paint
- green glow-in-the-dark acrylic paint
- plastic 1-gallon milk jug, rinsed
- utility knife
- small electric candle

abduct—to take someone away by force

Step 1: Paint the circle indents on the milk jug black. Paint the rest of the jug green. Let dry.

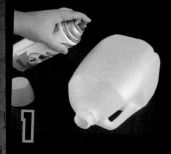

Step 2: Turn the jug over and set it on a hard surface so that the spout of the jug is on the bottom. Using black paint, make a single straight line for the alien's mouth.

Step 3: Have an adult cut a hole in the back of the jug with a utility knife. Turn on a mini electric candle and place it inside the hole. Set the jug on a flat surface.

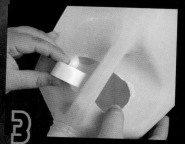

TIP: Not into aliens? Make Frankenstein's monster instead! Paint the jug dark green and use black paint to make the monster's face. Glue on some wiggle eyes. Paint two corks silver and hot glue them on each side of the head.

Floating Eyeballs

Are you in need of an eye-catching table decoration? Look no further! Dig around in the kitchen to find your ingredients. These spooky "eyeballs" will have your friends' stomachs rolling in no time.

What You Need:
- strainer
- 1 20-ounce (600-mL) can of **lychees**
- clear canister or jar
- small jar of green olives
- water
- 1 teaspoon (5 mL) ground coffee
- wooden spoon
- red food coloring

lychee—a small round fruit

Step 1: Using a strainer, drain the lychee juice into a canister.

Step 2: Stuff each lychee with a green olive. Make sure the red pimento in the middle of the olive faces out.

Step 3: Place the lychees in the canister with the juice.

Step 4: Fill the canister with water. Add coffee and stir lightly with the spoon. Position the "eyeballs" so they're looking out of the canister.

Step 5: Add a few drops of red food coloring to the canister. Do not stir. Let the red color run unevenly through the canister to make it look like blood.

TIP: Lychees are available in most major supermarkets in the Asian foods aisle. If you can't find them, use radishes instead. Peel each radish, leaving little bits of red skin to look like veins. Have an adult help you cut out a hole in the center of each radish. Stuff each radish with a green olive.

Buried Alive

What's that crawling out of the flowerpot? Look! It's a hand! This decoration will make your friends wonder what else is buried beneath the "dirt."

What You Need:

- medium-sized flowerpot
- glue gun and hot glue
- plastic bugs
- 1 package chocolate sandwich cookies, crushed
- newspaper, torn
- rubber glove
- rubber band
- white gauze, cut in long strips
- sponge brush
- acrylic paints
- gummy worms

TIP: For a completely edible twist on this tasty treat, use a plastic cauldron instead of a flowerpot. Add candy eyeballs and fingertips in place of the hand.

Step 1: Hot glue fake bugs onto the outside of the flowerpot.

Step 2: Fill the pot with crushed cookies and set aside.

Step 3: Stuff pieces of newspaper into a rubber glove. Tie off the end of the glove with a rubber band.

Step 4: Wrap gauze around the hand. Use hot glue to secure.

Step 5: Dab red paint on the hand with sponge brush wherever you'd like to add some "blood."

Step 6: Place the hand in the flowerpot. Bury the bottom of the hand in the cookies. Let the fingers hang over the side.

Step 7: Sprinkle gummy worms on top of the cookies.

Batty for Blood

Bloodsucking bats are on the prowl in this spooky project. The shadowy shapes hanging overhead will have your friends ducking for cover. If the beady eyes don't terrify them, the spooky fangs will. Chomp!

What You Need:
- scissors
- egg carton
- paintbrush
- black acrylic paint
- black cardstock
- glue gun and hot glue
- red construction paper
- white glue
- black gauze, torn into long strips
- black string or yarn

Step 1: Cut out one cup from an egg carton and paint it black. Let dry.

Step 2: Cut out bat wings from black cardstock. Keep the wings rounded at the top and jagged like the letter "M" at the bottom.

Step 3: Hot glue the bat wings to the sides of the egg cup.

Step 4: Cut out two pointed ears from black cardstock. Cut out two eyes and fangs from red construction paper. Glue the ears, eyes, and fangs to the egg cup.

Step 5: Hot glue the black gauze to the bat's wings. Let the gauze drape down the wings unevenly.

Step 6: Use the scissors to punch two holes in the bat. Thread a piece of string through the holes and tie the bat to a tree branch.

TIP: If you don't have trees in your yard, hang the bats inside the house. Ask an adult to hang them from the blades of a ceiling fan. Turn the fan on at a low speed and watch your bats zoom overhead.

Spooky Tabletop Spiders

These spooky spiders look like they're ready to crawl off the table. Place them around your house to make everyone feel like they're being watched.

What You Need:

- paintbrush
- black acrylic paint
- 1 foam ball, cut in half
- gold glitter acrylic p
- 4 black chenille ster
- 5 tinsel stems
- glue gun and hot gl
- 2 wiggle eyes
- 2 red pom-poms
- scissors

Step 1: Paint a foam ball with black paint. Let dry four hours.

Step 2: Paint over the black paint with gold glitter paint. Let dry two hours.

Step 3: Insert four stems into each side of the foam. Alternate between the black chenille and tinsel stems. Bend the ends of the stems to create feet. Bend the stems at the middle to make the knee joints.

Step 4: Hot glue wiggle eyes to the red pom-poms. Hot glue the pom-poms to the foam.

Step 5: Cut the extra tinsel stem in half. Fold each piece to make an "M" shape.

Step 6: Hot glue one M-shaped tinsel stem upside down above the pom-poms to make eyebrows. Hot glue the other M-shaped tinsel stem below the eyes to make fangs.

TIP: To change things up, paint the spider all black. Use only black chenille stems for the legs. Cut four pieces of red construction paper into triangles to make two red eyes and two fangs.

Zombie Witch

What's worse than a witch at your doorstep? A zombie witch who's hungry for human brains! Your friends won't guess that this creepy creature was made out of a broom and a milk jug.

What You Need:

- paintbrush
- acrylic paints
- plastic 1-gallon milk jug, rinsed
- glue gun and hot glue
- wiggle eyes
- tinfoil
- masking tape
- raisins
- black yarn, cut into 3-foot (0.9-m) pieces
- broomstick
- plastic rain poncho
- witch's hat

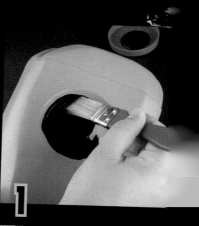

Step 1: Paint the circle indents on a milk jug black. Paint the rest of the jug gray. Let dry.

Step 2: Turn the jug over and set it on a hard surface so that the spout of the jug is on the bottom. Using black paint, paint a witch's mouth.

Step 3: Hot glue wiggle eyes to the black circles.

Turn to next page

Step 4: Shape tinfoil into a long, pointed witch's nose.

Step 5: Wrap nose with masking tape and paint gray. Let dry.

Step 6: Hot glue raisins to the nose to look like warts. Then hot glue the nose to the witch's face.

Step 7: Hot glue yarn onto the top of the milk carton. The yarn should fall over the sides of the jug.

Step 8: Place the witch's head on a broomstick. Lean the broomstick against a wall in a corner.

Step 9: Place a rain poncho on the witch. Let the hood cover the witch's head like a cloak.

Step 10: Put a witch's hat on top of her head.

TIP: If you don't have a witch's hat, make your own. Cut out two large circles from black construction paper. Roll one circle into a cone and glue to secure. Cut a hole the size of the cone bottom in the center of the second circle, leaving tabs. Glue the inside of the cone to the tabs.

Intestines in a Jar

Everyone will be grossed out when you set this "bloody" decoration on the table. Don't be surprised if your friends start counting heads to find out if anyone's missing.

What You Need:

- scissors
- 1 pair flesh-colored pantyhose
- newspaper
- clear canister or jar
- 2 32-ounce (930-mL) boxes red gelatin mix
- large liquid measuring cup
- saucepan
- 2 cups (480 mL) boiling water
- wooden spoon
- 2 cups (480 mL) cold water
- chunky salsa

Step 1: Cut the legs off a pair of pantyhose. Stuff each leg with crumpled newspaper. Tie off the ends of each leg.

Step 2: Place the stuffed pantyhose into a clear canister. Wrap them in circles until they look like coiled snakes.

Step 3: Empty the gelatin packets into a measuring cup.

Step 4: Have an adult boil 2 cups of water. Pour the boiling water over the gelatin mix and stir for one minute with the spoon. Add 2 cups of cold water and stir.

Step 5: Pour the gelatin mixture evenly over the stuffed pantyhose. Refrigerate for at least four hours.

Step 6: Remove canister from the refrigerator. Pour chunky salsa on top of the intestines.

TIP: Before you tie off the ends of the pantyhose, insert some fake bugs or rats. People will wonder what kind of creature the intestines came from!

Trash Bag Black Widows

With glowing red eyes, these black widows will turn an ordinary front yard into a nightmare. Friends will dare each other to step a little closer to this scary lawn creature.

What You Need:

- 18 large black trash bags
- dead leaves or old newspaper
- black electrical tape
- scissors
- clear glue
- red tissue paper
- 2 clear plastic cups
- white and red construction paper
- 2 mini flashlights

Step 1: Stuff one trash bag with dead leaves or crumpled newspaper. Tie the top of the bag into a knot and flip the bag upside down.

Step 2: Stuff another trash bag about 1/3 less than the first bag. Tie the top of the bag into a knot and flip the bag upside down. Use electrical tape to attach it to the front of the bigger bag.

Step 3: To make each leg, lay two trash bags flat, one on top of the other. Roll the bags lengthwise.

Turn to next page

Step 4: Use electrical tape to secure the tops and bottoms of each leg. Also use electrical tape in the center to make a leg joint. Repeat this process seven times for the rest of the legs.

Step 5: Cut four slits on each side of the larger trash bag. Insert one leg into each slit. Use electrical tape to secure.

Step 6: To make the eyes, glue a very thin sheet of red tissue paper around each plastic cup. Tape the open part of the cups to the head of the black widow. Leave room to insert the flashlights later.

TIP: Give your spider a home by turning cheesecloth into a spiderweb. Use your hands to gently stretch the cheesecloth. As it spreads, it begins to look like a spiderweb. Place the web under the spider or beside it.

4

5

6

Step 7: To make the fangs, cut white construction paper into two sharp triangles. Tape to the head under the eyes.

Step 8: Cut a large piece of red construction paper into an hourglass shape. Tape onto the top of the back of the spider.

Step 9: Place a mini flashlight into each cup. Now you have a black widow with glowing eyes!

Glossary

abduct (ab-DUKT)—to take someone away by force

cauldron (KAWL-druhn)—a large kettle

edible (ED-uh-buhl)—able to be eaten

gelatin (JEL-uh-tuhn)—a clear substance used in making jelly and desserts

intestine (in-TESS-tin)—one of the long, hollow tubes below the stomach

lychee (LY-chee)—a small, round fruit that has a red outer covering and sweet white flesh surrounding a seed

Read More

Bell-Rehwoldt, Sheri. *The Kids' Guide to Building Cool Stuff.* Kids' Guides. Mankato, Minn.: Capstone Press, 2009.

McGee, Randel. *Paper Crafts for Halloween.* Paper Craft Fun for Holidays. Berkeley Heights, N.J.: Enslow Elementary, 2009.

Schuette, Sarah. *How to Carve Freakishly Cool Pumpkins.* Halloween Extreme. Mankato, Minn.: Capstone Press, 2011.

Skillicorn, Helen. *Spooky Crafts.* Creative Crafts for Kids. New York: Gareth Stevens Pub., 2010.

Internet Sites

FactHound offers a safe, fun way to find Internet sites related to this book. All of the sites on FactHound have been researched by our staff.

Here's all you do:

Visit *www.facthound.com*

Type in this code: 9781429654234

Check out projects, games and lots more at
www.capstonekids.com

Index